Let the Adventure Begin

Date of Departure _______________

Destination

____

PACKING LIST

ESSENTIALS

- [ ] ID
- [ ] CARDS
- [ ] PHONE
- [ ] BOOKING DETAILS
- [ ] CAMERA

TOILETRIES

- [ ] TOOTHBRUSH
- [ ] TOOTHPASTE
- [ ] SUNSCREEN
- [ ] DEODORANT
- [ ] HAIRBRUSH

CLOTHING

- [ ] 3 DAYS OUTFITS
- [ ] COMFY SHOES
- [ ] FANCY SHOES
- [ ] UNDERCLOTHES
- [ ] JACKET
- [ ] PJ'S
- [ ] SHADES

Outfit Planner

Day ____________ Weather____________

Day Plans ____________________________

Top(s)________________________________

Bottom _______________________________

Shoes ________________________________

Accessories___________________________

Night Plans___________________________

Top(s) ________________________________

Bottom _______________________________

Shoes ________________________________

Accessories ___________________________

Day ____________ Weather____________

Day Plans ____________________________

Top(s)________________________________

Bottom _______________________________

Shoes ________________________________

Accessories___________________________

Night Plans___________________________

Top(s) ________________________________

Bottom _______________________________

Shoes ________________________________

Accessories ___________________________

Day ____________ Weather____________

Day Plans ____________________________

Top(s)________________________________

Bottom _______________________________

Shoes ________________________________

Accessories___________________________

Night Plans___________________________

Top(s) ________________________________

Bottom _______________________________

Shoes ________________________________

Accessories ___________________________

Day ____________ Weather____________

Day Plans ____________________________

Top(s)________________________________

Bottom _______________________________

Shoes ________________________________

Accessories___________________________

Night Plans___________________________

Top(s) ________________________________

Bottom _______________________________

Shoes ________________________________

Accessories ___________________________

Outfit Planner

Day _________ Weather _________
Day Plans _________________________
Top(s) _____________________________
Bottom _____________________________
Shoes ______________________________
Accessories ________________________
Night Plans ________________________
Top(s) _____________________________
Bottom _____________________________
Shoes ______________________________
Accessories ________________________

Day _________ Weather _________
Day Plans _________________________
Top(s) _____________________________
Bottom _____________________________
Shoes ______________________________
Accessories ________________________
Night Plans ________________________
Top(s) _____________________________
Bottom _____________________________
Shoes ______________________________
Accessories ________________________

Day _________ Weather _________
Day Plans _________________________
Top(s) _____________________________
Bottom _____________________________
Shoes ______________________________
Accessories ________________________
Night Plans ________________________
Top(s) _____________________________
Bottom _____________________________
Shoes ______________________________
Accessories ________________________

Day _________ Weather _________
Day Plans _________________________
Top(s) _____________________________
Bottom _____________________________
Shoes ______________________________
Accessories ________________________
Night Plans ________________________
Top(s) _____________________________
Bottom _____________________________
Shoes ______________________________
Accessories ________________________

TRIP PLANNER

CHECKLIST

PLACES TO EAT

THINGS TO SEE

TRAVEL DETAILS

NOTES

TRIP PLANNER

CHECKLIST

PLACES TO EAT

THINGS TO SEE

TRAVEL DETAILS

NOTES

MILEAGE LOG

MAKE:	MODEL:	YEAR:

DATE:	ODOMETER: START | END	TOTAL:	DESTINATION / PURPOSE:

MILEAGE LOG

MAKE:		MODEL:		YEAR:
DATE:	**ODOMETER:** **START | END**		**TOTAL:**	**DESTINATION /** **PURPOSE:**

Check Fluids
Tires
lights
horn
Riding Gear
Forcast
Rainsuit
Water proof gloves
Map
Spare Key
Tool kit

Travel Tracker

Where I've been...	Where I want to go next

Choose or Flip a Coin

TRAVEL EDITION

CITY / BEACH

MORNING / NIGHTTIME

DINNER / COCKTAILS

EUROPE / ASIA

LUXURY / BACKPACKING

RESTAURANT / STREET FOOD

Plane / BOAT

PLANNING / IMPROVISE

SUN / SNOW

SHOPPING / ATTRACTIONS

Weekly Planner

Monday

Tuesday

Wednesday

Thursday

Friday

Saturday

Sunday

to-do

Notes

Weekly Planner

Monday

Tuesday

Wednesday

Thursday

Friday

Saturday

Sunday

to-do

Notes

Month: **Year:**

Date:	Description Of Expense:	Payment Type:	Amount:

TRIP WEATHER LOG

TRIP WEATHER LOG

TRIP WEATHER LOG

COFFEE
Coffee

COFFEE NAME _______________________   DATE _______________________

BEVERAGE _______________________

PLACE TASTED _______________________   PRICE _______________________

COUNTRY / REGION _______________________

COMPANY _______________________

TESTING RATING

	0.5	1	1.5	2	2.5	3	3.5	4	4.5	5
APPEARANCE										
AROMA										
FLAVOR										

	0.5	1	1.5	2	2.5	3	3.5	4	4.5	5
SWEET										
ACIDIC										
SPICY										
CITRUS										
CHOCOLATE										
CARAMEL										
BITTER										
SAVORY										

BREW METHOD

DRIP ☐   ESPRESSO ☐   PRESS ☐

POUR-OVER ☐   SIPHON ☐   OTHER _______

NOTES _______________________

____

____

____

____

____

____

____

RECOMMEND TO _______________________

____

____

____

____

____

____

____

COFFEE NAME ________________________________   DATE ________________

BEVERAGE ________________________________

PLACE TASTED ________________________________   PRICE ________________

COUNTRY / REGION ________________________________

COMPANY ________________________________

TESTING RATING

	0.5	1	1.5	2	2.5	3	3.5	4	4.5	5
APPEARANCE										
AROMA										
FLAVOR										

	0.5	1	1.5	2	2.5	3	3.5	4	4.5	5
SWEET										
ACIDIC										
SPICY										
CITRUS										
CHOCOLATE										
CARAMEL										
BITTER										
SAVORY										

BREW METHOD

DRIP ☐   ESPRESSO ☐   PRESS ☐

POUR-OVER ☐   SIPHON ☐   OTHER ____________

NOTES ________________________________

RECOMMEND TO ________________

____

____

____

____

____

____

____

____

Wine

Vintage

grapes

% alcohol

producer

country-region

perfect pairing

serving temperature

suggested glass

price

wine-tasting

when

where

with

appearance

nose

taste

opinion

notes and additional thoughts

rating:

Wine

Vintage

grapes

% alcohol

producer

country-region

perfect pairing

serving temperature

suggested glass

price

wine-tasting

when

where

with

appearance

nose

taste

opinion

notes and additional thoughts

rating:

MY TRIP TO

____

WHAT I WAS EXCITED FOR:

HOW I GOT THERE:

WHAT I SAW THERE:

MY FAVORITE PARTS OF THE TRIP:

WHAT I LEARNED:

WHAT SURPRISED ME THE MOST

MY TRIP TO

____

____

WHAT I WAS EXCITED FOR:

____

HOW I GOT THERE:

____

WHAT I SAW THERE:

____

MY FAVORITE PARTS OF THE TRIP:

____

WHAT I LEARNED:

____

WHAT SURPRISED ME THE MOST

____

A GOOD iDEA BECOMES A GREAT iDEA WHEN YOU LET iT OUT!

add notes, pictures, or postcards

add notes, pictures, or postcards

add notes, pictures, or postcards

Add notes, pictures, or postcards

add notes, pictures, or postcards

add notes, pictures, or postcards

Shopping List

Name:

Name:

Name:

Name:

Shopping List

Name:

Name:

Name:

Name:

Shopping List

Name:

Name:

Name:

Name:

attach postcards here

Carte Postale
Fabrication Française
P.C
PARIS

attach postcards here

attach postcards here

Travel Buddies

Travel Buddies

Travel Buddies

Travel Buddies

From Here to There

From Here to There

From Here to There

Trip Journal

Trip Journal

Trip Journal

Trip Journal

Trip Journal

Trip Journal

Trip Journal

Trip Journal

Trip Journal

Trip Journal

Recipes Found Along the Way

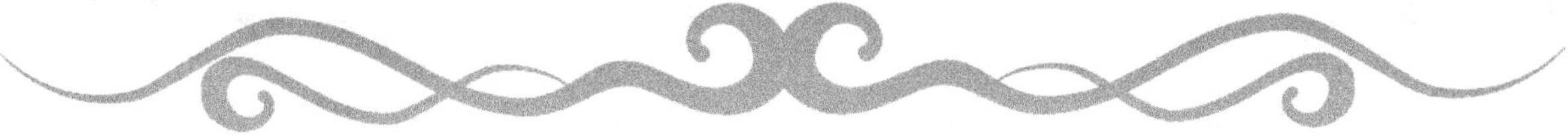

RECIPE:

INGREDIENTS:

COOKING INSTRUCTIONS:

NOTES:

RECIPE:

INGREDIENTS:

COOKING INSTRUCTIONS:

NOTES:

RECIPE:

INGREDIENTS:

COOKING INSTRUCTIONS:

NOTES:

RECIPE:

INGREDIENTS:

COOKING INSTRUCTIONS:

NOTES:

RECIPE:

INGREDIENTS:

COOKING INSTRUCTIONS:

NOTES:

RECIPE:

INGREDIENTS:

COOKING INSTRUCTIONS:

NOTES:

MOVIES

Movie title:

Director:

Genre: **Year:**

Date Watched :

Rating: ☆ ☆ ☆ ☆ ☆

Cast:

Review:

Notes:

Movie title:

Director:

Genre: **Year:**

Date Watched :

Rating: ☆ ☆ ☆ ☆ ☆

Cast:

Review:

Notes:

Movie title:

Director:

Genre: **Year:**

Date Watched :

Rating: ☆ ☆ ☆ ☆ ☆

Cast:

Review:

Notes:

Movie title:

Director:

Genre: **Year:**

Date Watched :

Rating: ☆ ☆ ☆ ☆ ☆

Cast:

Review:

Notes:

Cities We Visited

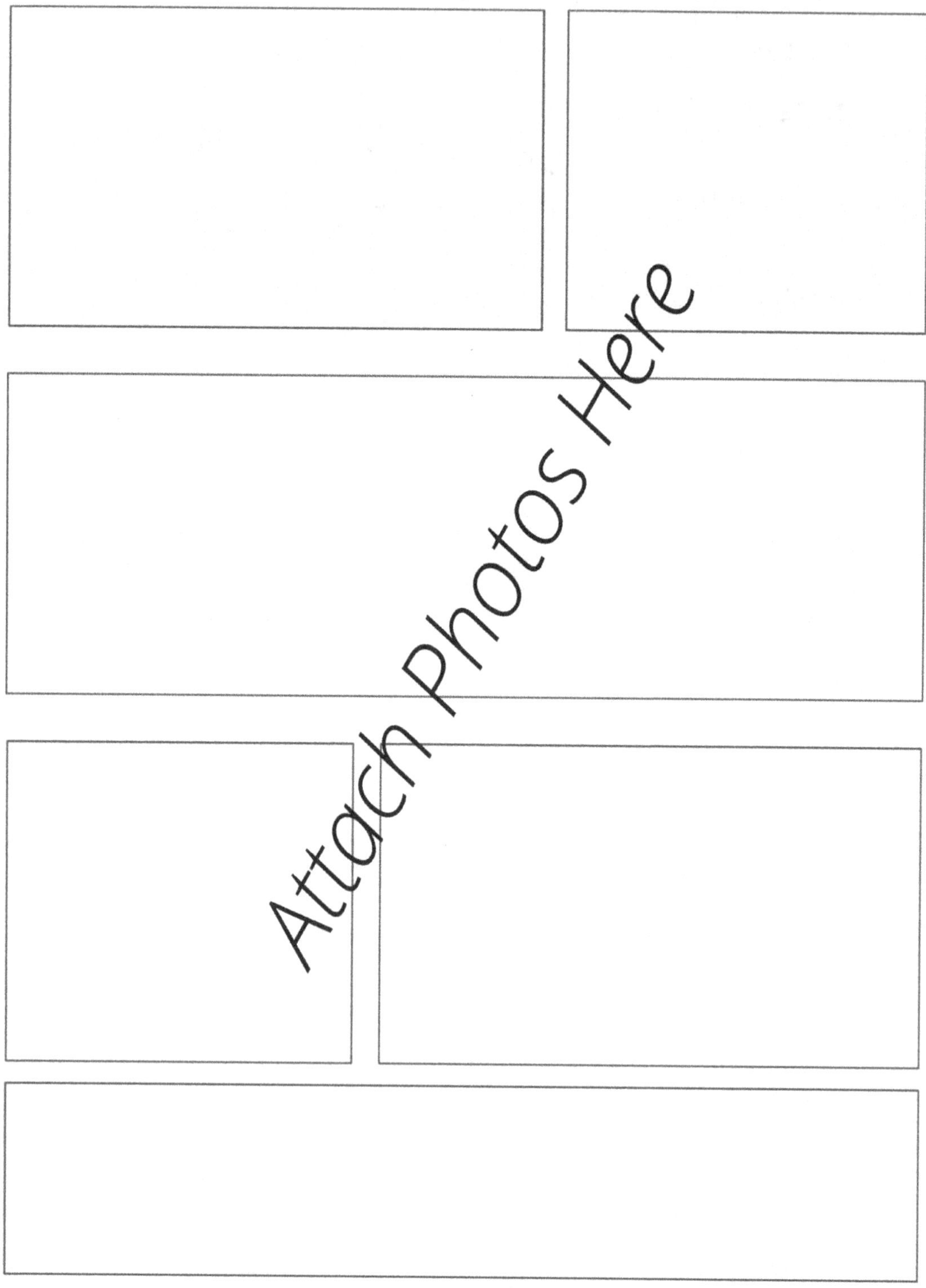

Cities We Visited

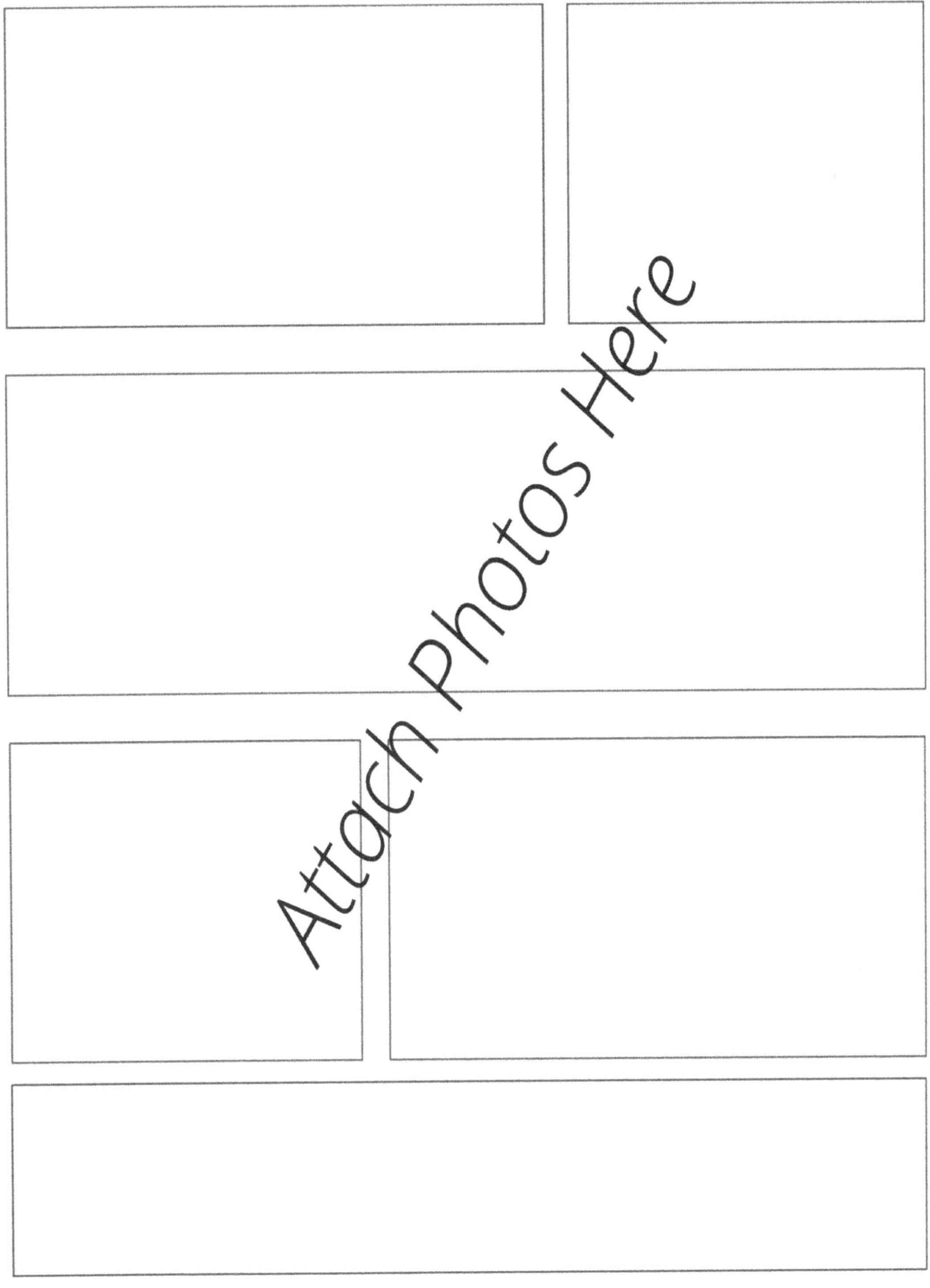

Cities We Visited

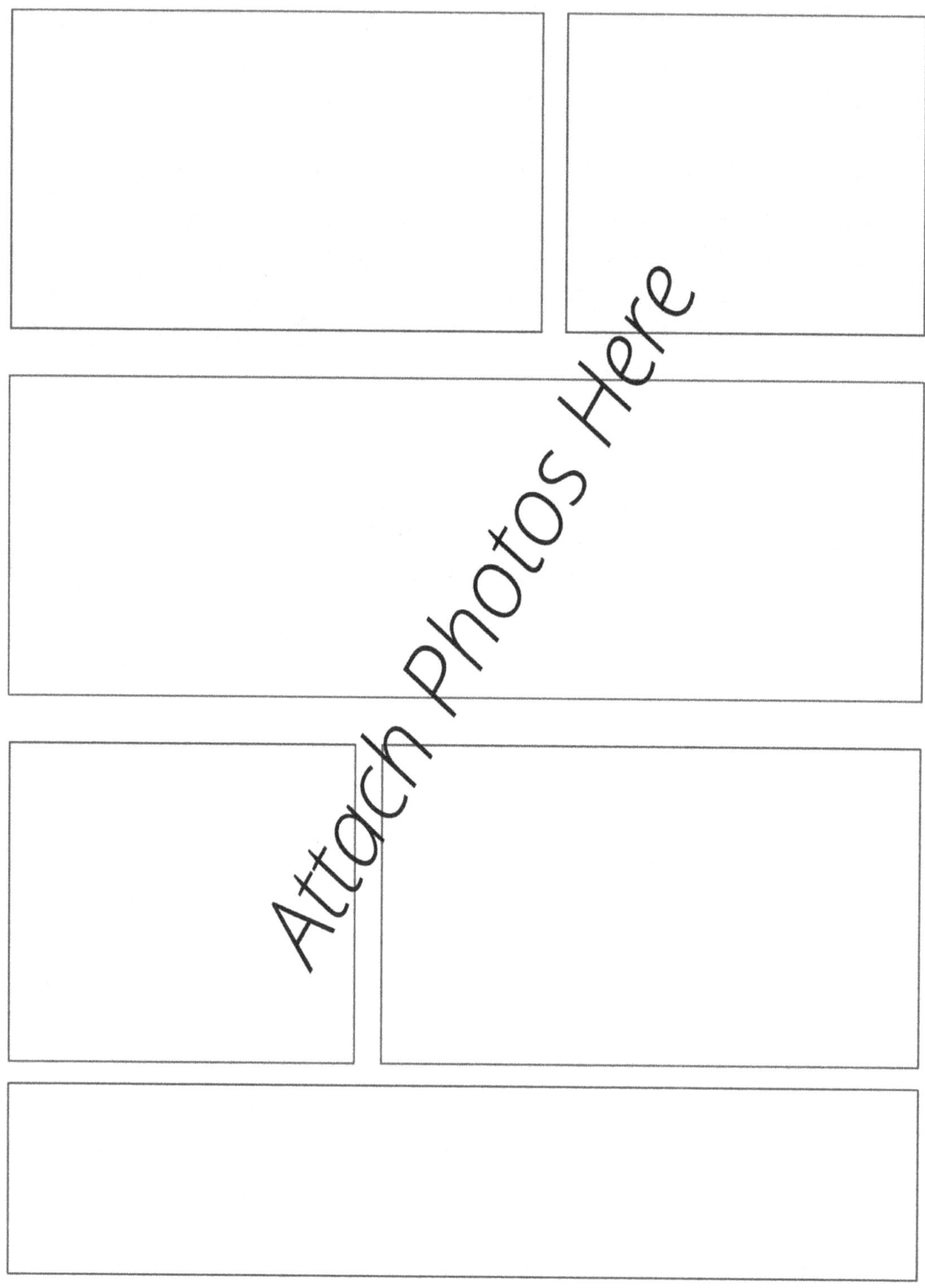

Cities We Visited

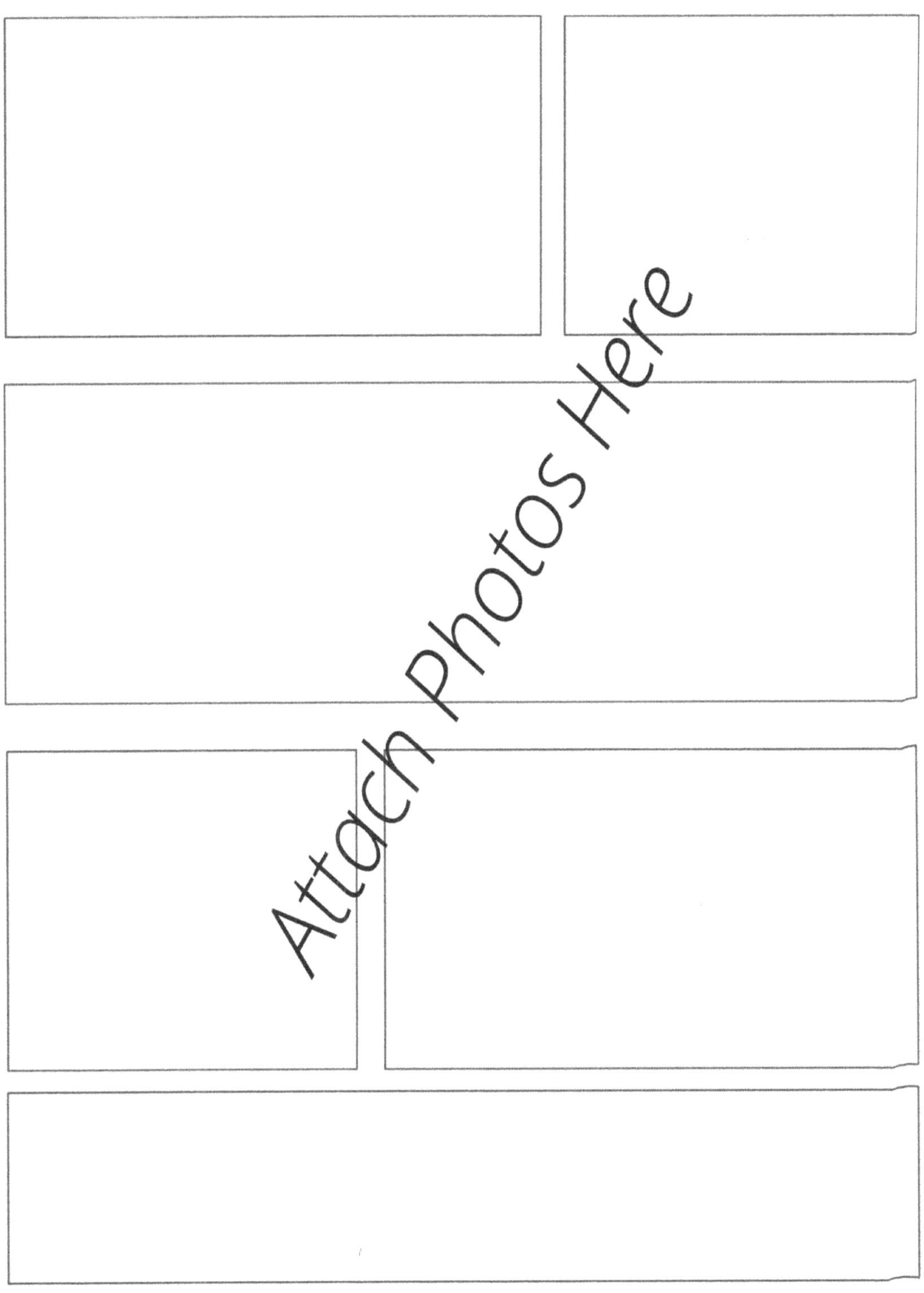

Cities We Visited

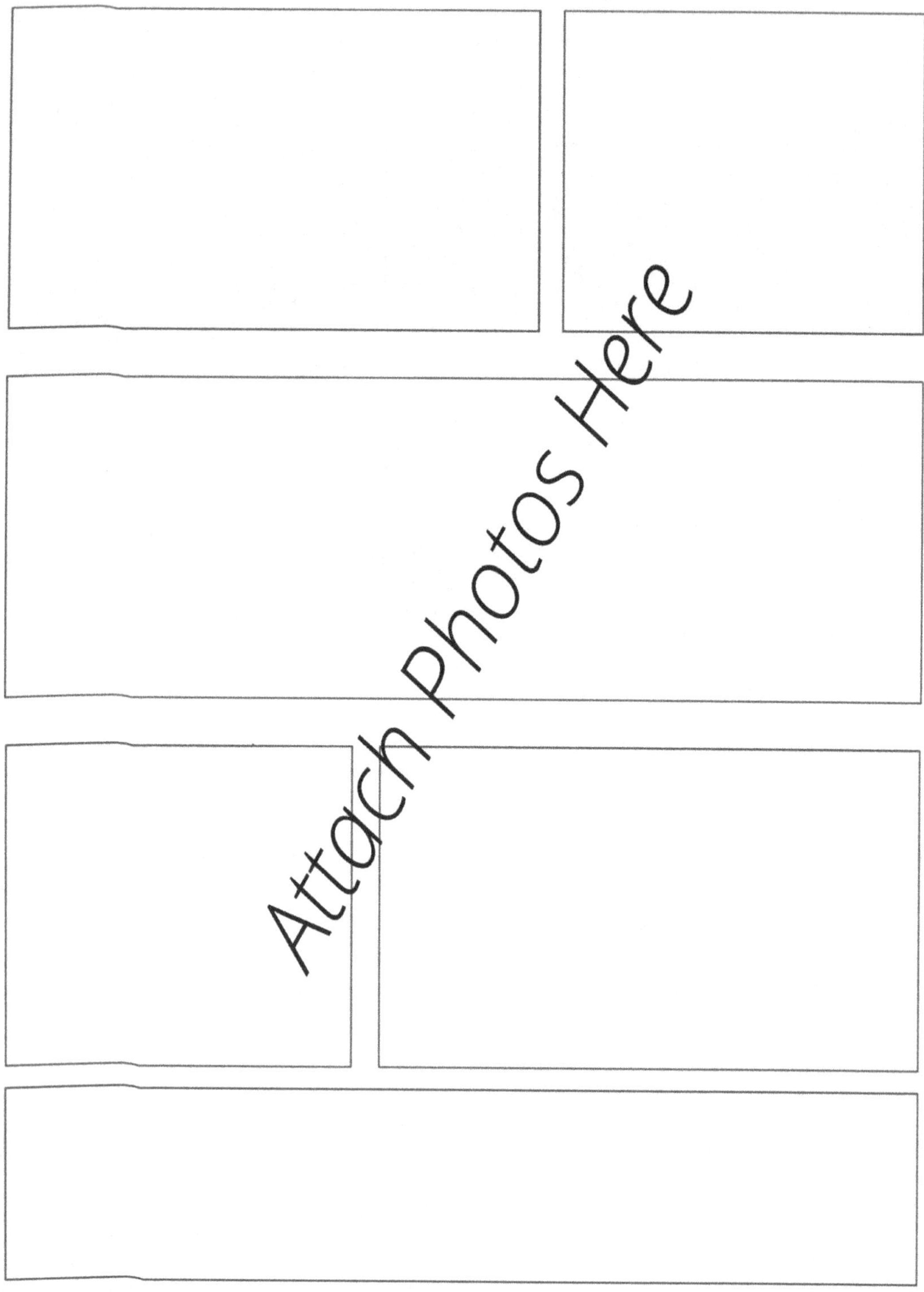

Cities We Visited

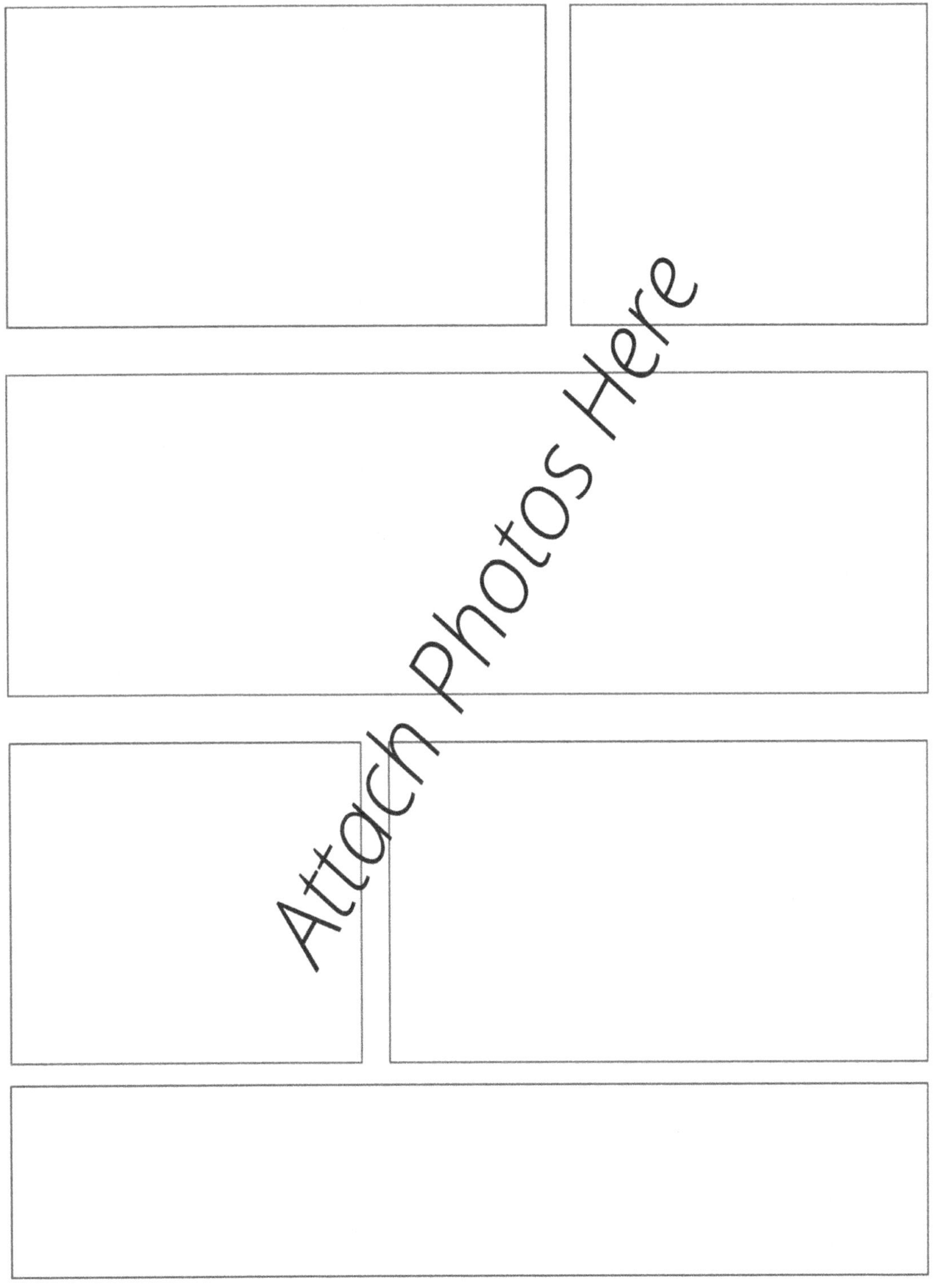

Cities We Visited

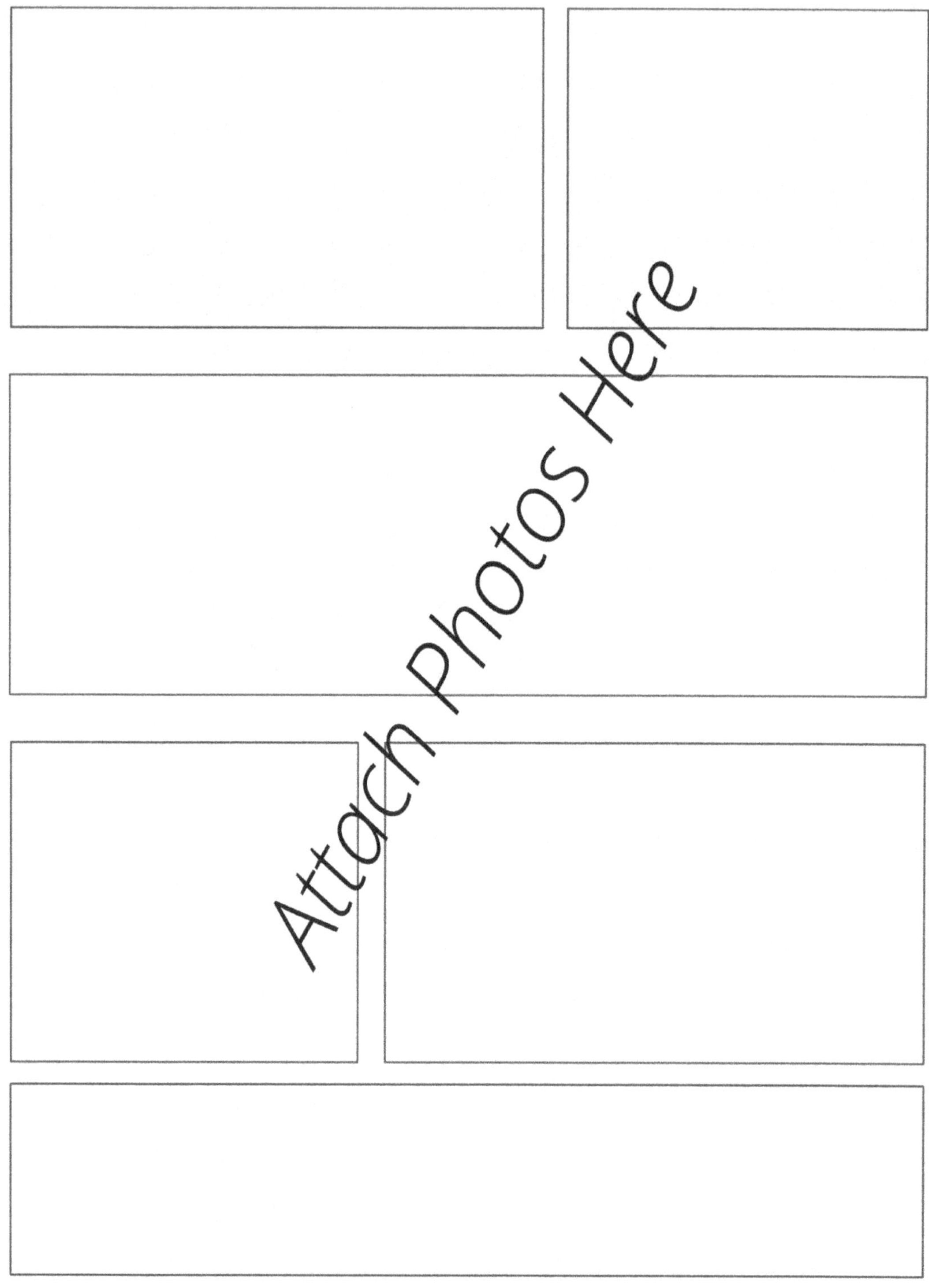

Cities We Visited

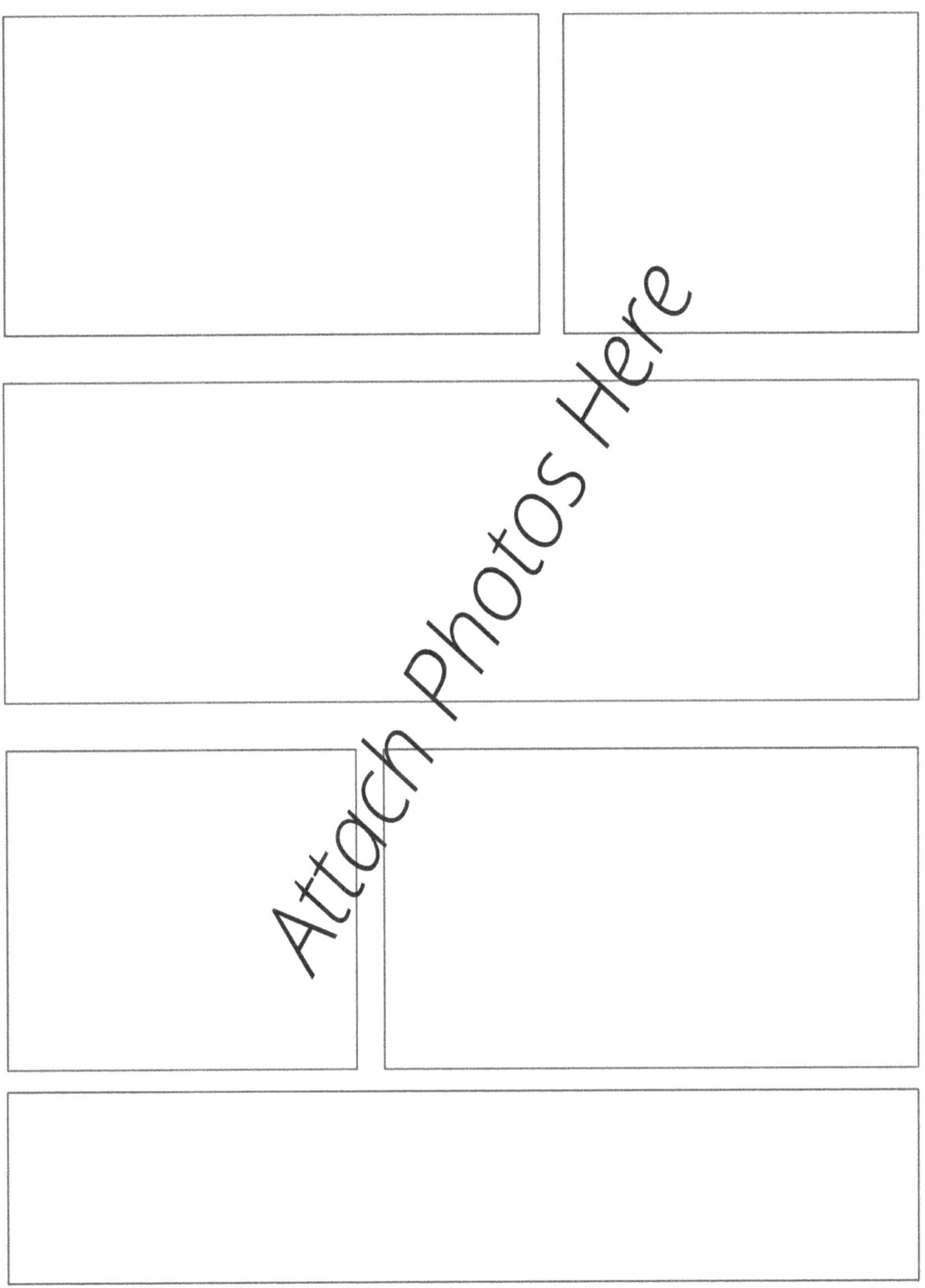

Cities We Visited

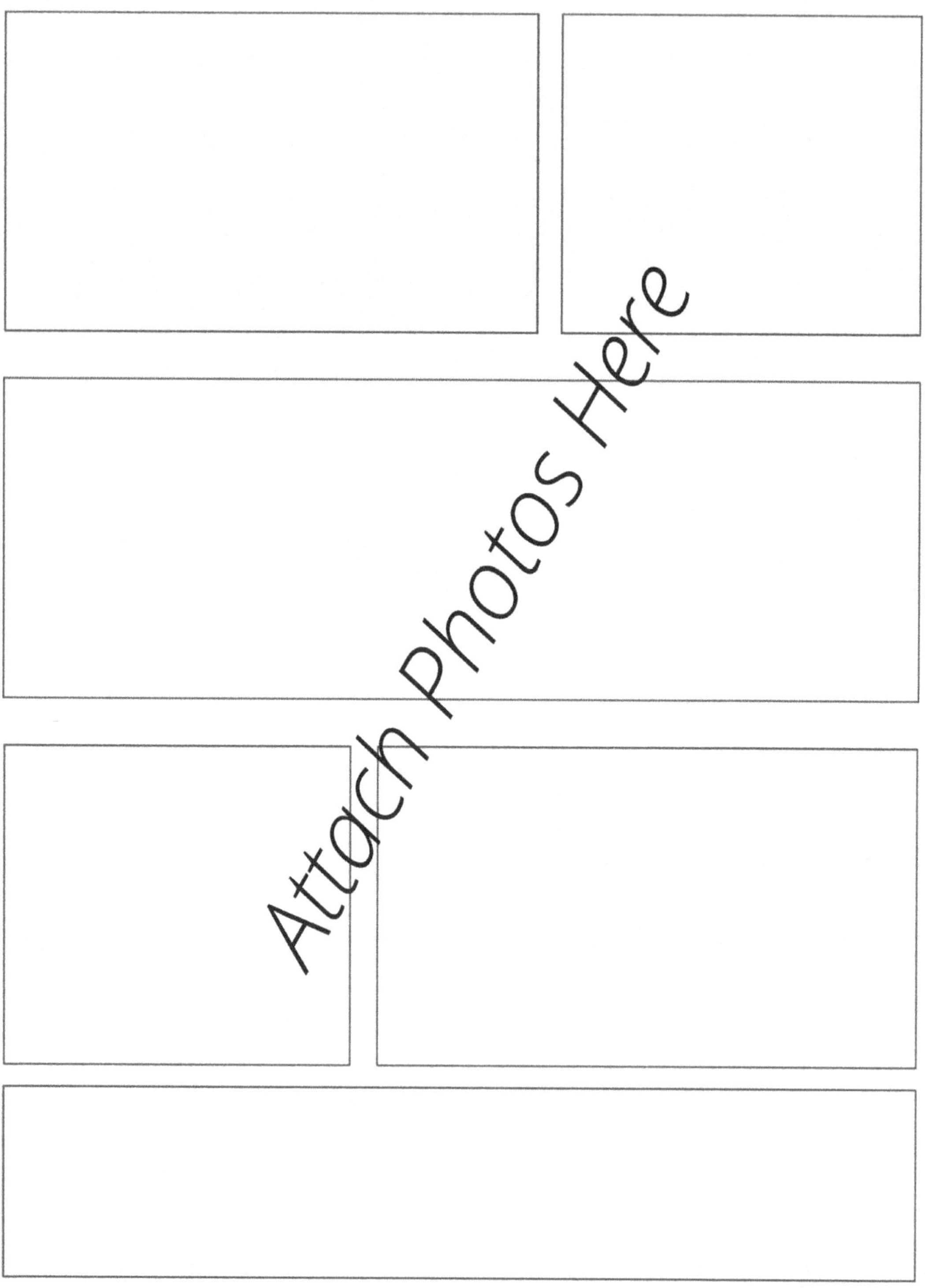

Travel Poster

CLOSED
FOR VACATION
RETURN DATE

Hotels we stayed in

Gas prices along the way

Please wait...

I'm thinking!

Problems along the Way

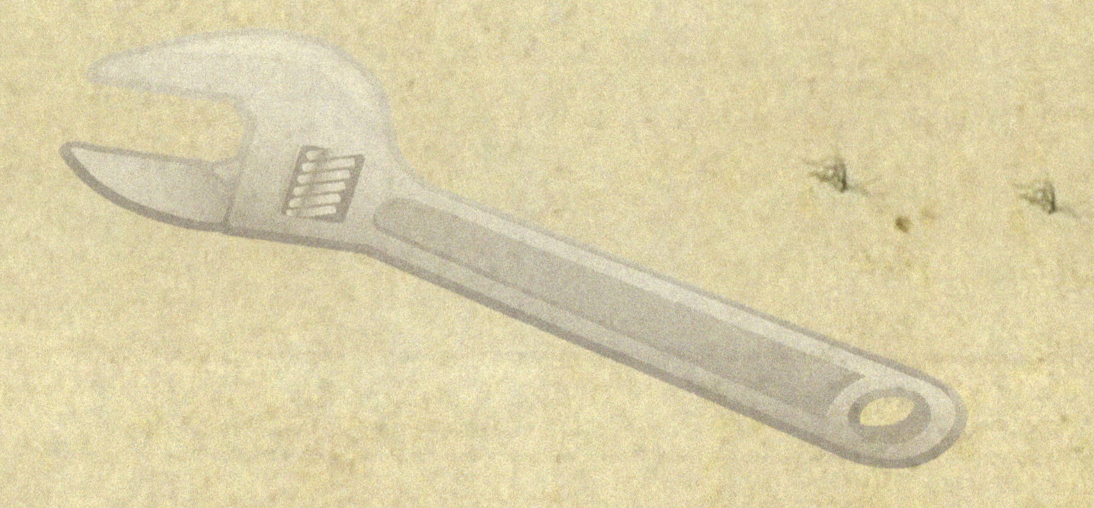

What's
Next?

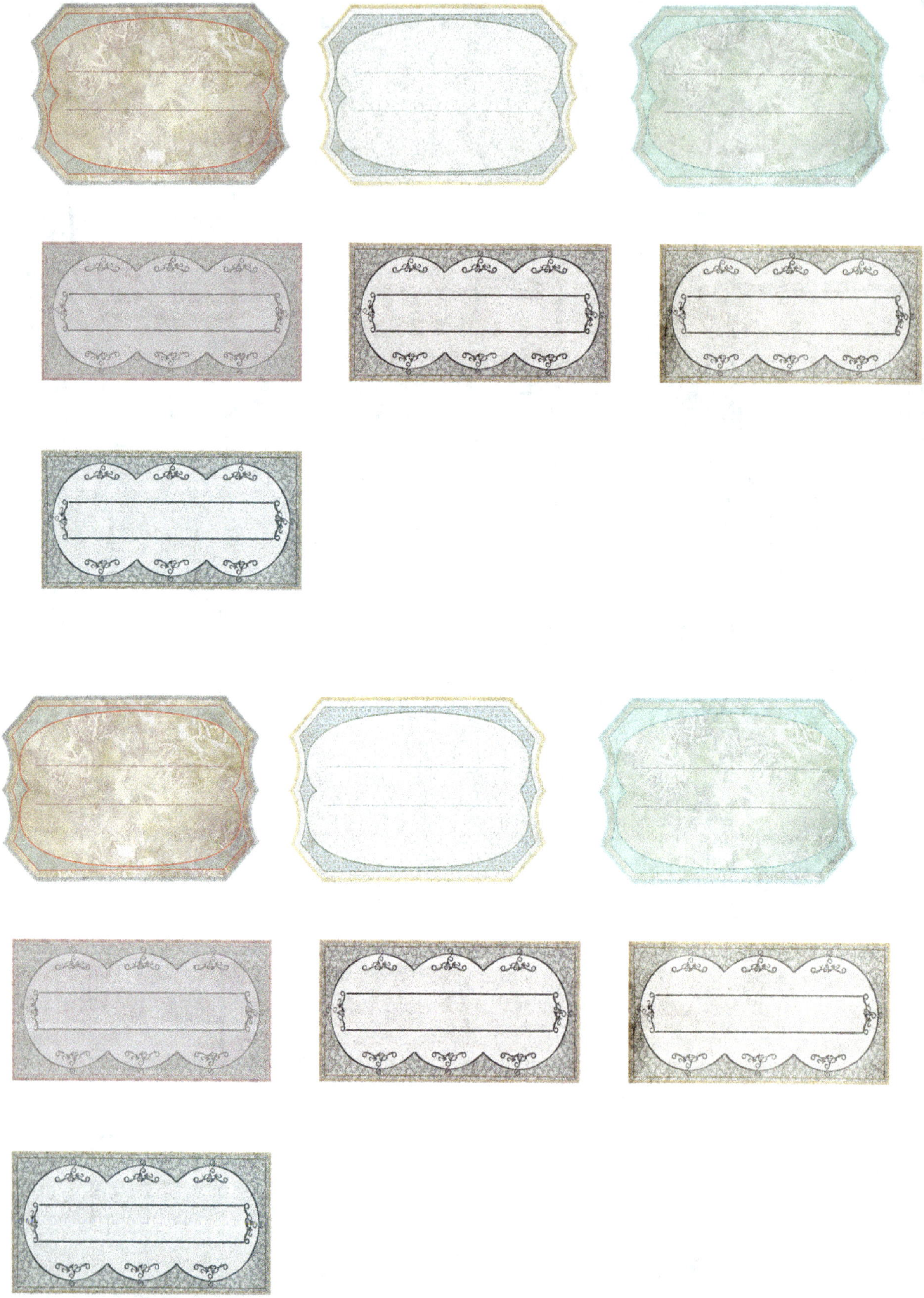

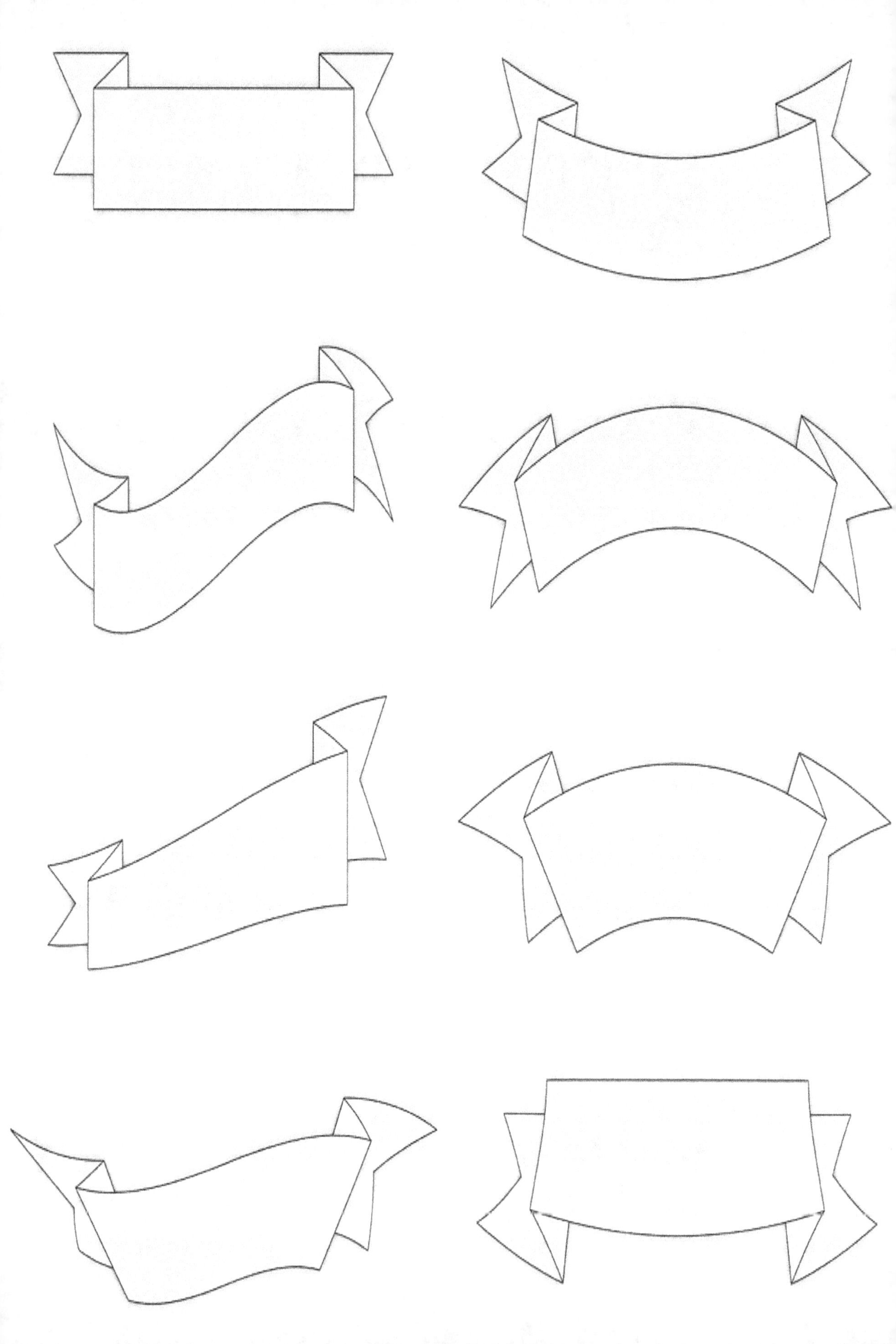

Tbrad Designs